Christmas Cookbook

Guilt-Free Festive Recipes to Celebrate and Stay Fit

LISA SHARON

Table Of Contents

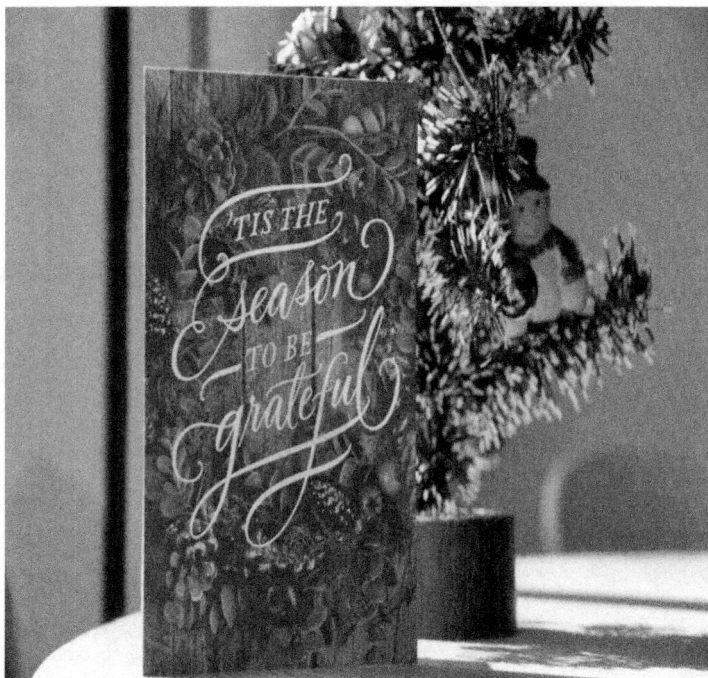

Introduction

A Gift of Health This Christmas

Dear Friend,

If you've picked up this book, you're probably feeling that familiar holiday anxiety. You know the one – where excitement about Christmas festivities mingles with worry about undoing all your hard-earned health progress. **Maybe you're remembering last year's New Year's resolution to "do better"** after another season of overindulgence, or perhaps you're tired of entering January feeling sluggish and disappointed.

I see you. And you're not alone.
This cookbook isn't just another collection of low-calorie holiday recipes. It's your permission slip to truly enjoy Christmas while

caring for your wellbeing. Whether you're a busy parent trying to create healthy traditions for your family, someone on a weight loss journey, or simply looking to maintain your healthy lifestyle through the festive season – you've found your companion for the holidays.

Why This Cookbook Is Different

Let's be honest – most "diet" cookbooks strip away everything that makes Christmas food special. Not this one. Instead of asking you to sacrifice tradition, we're reimagining it. Every recipe in this book has been crafted to honor those cherished holiday flavors while nourishing your body. We're not just cutting calories; we're enhancing nutrition, satisfaction, and joy.

The Science Behind Festive Weight Management

Did you know your body actually craves heartier foods during winter months? It's not just you – it's biology. But here's the exciting part: understanding this science lets us work with our bodies, not against them. Through these pages, you'll discover how to harness natural hunger cues, manage portion sizes without feeling deprived, and make choices that keep you energized through the busy holiday season.

How to Use This Book

Think of this cookbook as your flexible holiday companion, not a strict rulebook. Each chapter builds on the last, but feel free to jump to what you need most right now. Every recipe includes:

- Clear prep times and difficulty levels

- Make-ahead tips for busy days
- Nutritional information that actually matters
- Variations to suit different dietary needs
- Real-life tips for social situations

Your Holiday Wellness Promise

This Christmas can be different. I promise you won't find any bland "diet food" here. No cardboard-tasting cookies or sad salads.
Instead, you're about to discover how to:
- Create gorgeous holiday meals that energize instead of drain you
- Navigate family gatherings with confidence
- Start January feeling proud instead of regretful
- Build traditions that blend health with celebration

Remember, this journey isn't about perfection. It's about finding joy in nourishing yourself while fully embracing the magic of the season. Your path to a healthier holiday starts here, and I'll be with you every step of the way.

Let's make this Christmas one where you feel truly merry, bright, and empowered.

With warmth and wellness,
[Lisa Sharon]

Chapter 1

The Psychology of Holiday Eating

Let's Picture this: You're standing in your grandmother's kitchen, surrounded by the familiar scents of cinnamon and vanilla. Before you even taste anything, memories flood back – childhood Christmases, family gatherings, moments of pure joy. This isn't just about food; it's about emotion, tradition, and connection. And that's exactly where our journey to healthier holiday eating begins.

Understanding Emotional Eating During Festivities

The holiday season creates a perfect storm for emotional eating. **Let's explore why:**

The Memory Connection

Your brain forms powerful associations between foods and memories. That gingerbread isn't just a cookie – it's your mother's smile as she decorated them with you. Understanding these connections is your first step toward mindful choices.

Holiday Stress and Food

Did you know cortisol (our stress hormone) peaks during the holiday season? This biological response can drive us toward comfort foods. But here's the good news: awareness of this pattern gives us the power to respond differently. **Try this simple exercise:**

> Emotion Check-In
> Before reaching for that extra helping, pause and ask:
> - Am I hungry, or am I feeling stressed?
> - What else might help me feel better right now?
> - How do I want to feel after eating?

Social Pressure and Family Dynamics

"Just one more piece – I made it specially!" Sound familiar? Family food-pushing comes from love, but it can derail our best intentions. Let's explore gentle ways to handle these situations while preserving relationships.

Mindful Eating Techniques for Holiday Gatherings

Transform your holiday eating experience with these practical strategies:

The 5-Sense Method
Before taking your first bite at any holiday meal:
1. **Look:** Appreciate the colors on your plate
2. **Smell:** Inhale the festive aromas
3. **Touch:** Notice textures
4. **Listen:** To the sounds around you
5. **Taste:** Take small, deliberate bites

This isn't just about slowing down – research shows mindful eating can reduce overall consumption by up to 30% while increasing satisfaction.

Practical Party Strategies
- Position yourself away from the buffet table
- Use the "talk first, plate second" rule at gatherings
- Master the art of the polite "no, thank you"

Creating New, Healthy Christmas Traditions

Let's reimagine holiday traditions through a wellness lens:

Movement-Based Memories
- Start a Christmas morning walk tradition
- Create an active advent calendar
- Turn holiday music into dance breaks

Kitchen Adventures

Replace cookie-only baking sessions with:
- Festive smoothie-making competitions
- Healthy food gift preparation
- Family recipe makeover challenges

Setting Realistic Holiday Fitness Goals

The key word here is realistic. Your holiday fitness plan should energize you, not exhaust you.

The 80/20 Approach

Aim for 80% mindful choices, allowing 20% for pure celebration. This isn't about mathematical precision – it's about sustainable balance.

SMART Holiday Goals

Instead of vague promises, try:
- **Specific:** "I'll walk 15 minutes after holiday meals"
- **Measurable:** Track your movement and energy levels

- **Achievable:** Plan around your actual schedule
- **Relevant:** Choose activities you enjoy
- **Time-bound:** Set daily or weekly mini-goals

Your Success Strategy
Create your personal holiday wellness map:
1. Identify your typical triggers
2. Plan specific responses
3. Choose support people
4. Set up environment for success

Remember This
The goal isn't to resist every temptation or never indulge. It's about building a conscious, joyful relationship with holiday food that leaves you feeling energized and proud. Your holiday eating story is yours to write – and it can include both health and happiness.

Let's move forward to Chapter 2, where we'll explore exactly how to transform those beloved holiday recipes into healthier versions – without losing an ounce of joy.

Chapter 2

Smart Swaps - Transforming Christmas Classics

Ever wondered how some people manage to enjoy all their favorite holiday dishes while maintaining their health goals? The secret lies not in deprivation, but in clever modifications that preserve the soul of traditional recipes while enhancing their nutritional profile. Let's unlock these secrets together.

The Science of Recipe Modification

Think of recipe modification as an art backed by science. When we understand how ingredients interact, we can create healthier versions of classics that don't just taste good – they taste authentic.

Understanding Flavor Profiles

The magic of Christmas recipes often comes from five key elements: sweetness, richness, spice, texture, and aroma. When modifying recipes, we need to maintain these elements while improving nutrition. For instance, that rich mouthfeel you love in creamy dishes doesn't actually come from heavy cream – it comes from fat molecules coating your tongue. We can recreate this sensation using healthier fats like pureed cashews or cauliflower.

The Role of Temperature and Texture

Have you noticed how warm foods taste sweeter? This scientific fact allows us to reduce sugar in hot beverages and baked goods while maintaining perceived sweetness. Similarly, adding air through whipping or using ingredients with natural bulk can create satisfying textures with fewer calories.

Healthy Ingredient Substitutions Guide

Let's explore some genius swaps that will revolutionize your holiday cooking:

For Baking

Instead of cups of refined sugar, try:

- Mashed ripe bananas for natural sweetness and moisture
- Pure vanilla extract to enhance perceived sweetness
- Unsweetened applesauce for moisture and fiber
- Greek yogurt for richness and protein boost

For Creamy Dishes
Skip heavy cream and try:
- Pureed cauliflower (steamed and blended until silky)
- Cashew cream (raw cashews soaked and blended)
- Greek yogurt mixed with herbs
- Silken tofu for protein-rich smoothness

For Rich Main Dishes
Transform traditional proteins by:
- Using herbs and spices to amplify flavor without added fats
- Brining lean meats to maintain moisture
- Incorporating umami-rich ingredients like mushrooms
- Adding roasted vegetables for depth and nutrition

Portion Control Without Feeling Deprived

The secret to satisfaction isn't just about how much you eat – it's about how you eat it. Here's your guide to feeling fulfilled with right-sized portions:

The Power of Plating

Ever noticed how the same amount of food looks different on various plate sizes? Your brain processes

portion size relative to plate size. Use this to your advantage by:
- Choosing 9-inch plates instead of 12-inch ones
- Serving rich dishes in ramekins
- Using tall, narrow glasses for caloric drinks

The Satisfaction Strategy
Create meals that truly satisfy by incorporating:
- Different textures in every meal
- A balance of protein, fiber, and healthy fats
- Mindful eating practices
- Strategic use of holiday spices

Essential Kitchen Tools for Healthy Holiday Cooking

Equipping your kitchen with the right tools makes healthy cooking effortless. Here are the must-haves:
For Precision
A good kitchen scale helps control portions while ensuring recipe success. Think of it as your silent partner in healthy cooking.
For Texture
A high-quality blender becomes your secret weapon for creating creamy textures without cream. Use it for everything from smoothies to sauce bases.

For Even Cooking

Invest in good non-stick pans and silicone baking mats. They'll help you reduce or eliminate added fats while achieving perfect results.

For Portion Control

Keep measuring cups and spoons handy, but also learn visual portion cues: a serving of protein should be about the size of your palm, while a portion of complex carbs should be about the size of your fist.

Remember, these modifications aren't about restriction – they're about enhancement. By making smart swaps, you're not just cutting calories; you're adding nutrition, creating more digestible dishes, and often improving the original recipes. The best part? Your family might not even notice the difference, except that they feel better after eating.

Let these tools and techniques be your foundation for creating holiday meals that honor both tradition and health. In the next chapter, we'll put these principles into practice with specific recipes that will become your new holiday staples.

Ready to start transforming your holiday favorites? Let's move on to some practical applications of these principles in your cooking.

Your Action Plan

1. Choose one favorite recipe to transform this week
2. Stock up on your top 3 substitute ingredients
3. Experiment with portion sizes using the visual guide
4. Set up your kitchen for success with essential tools

Next up in Chapter 3, we'll put these principles into action with specific breakfast recipes that will fuel your holiday morning without weighing you down.

Chapter 3

Jolly Breakfast & Brunch Options

There's something enchanting about Christmas morning that deserves more than just another breakfast. Today, I'm sharing recipes that have delighted families for generations – but with a healthy twist that'll keep you energized through every gift opening and festive moment.

Quick Pre-Gift Opening Energizers

When excitement fills the air and patience runs thin, these quick bites will keep everyone happy without spending hours in the kitchen.

Merry Berry Protein Balls

The perfect grab-and-go breakfast that tastes like a treat but fuels like a champion.

What You'll Need:

1 cup rolled oats

1/3 cup vanilla protein powder

1/4 cup almond butter

3 tablespoons honey

1/2 teaspoon cinnamon

1/4 cup dried cranberries

1/4 cup mini dark chocolate chips

2-3 tablespoons almond milk

How to Make Magic:

1. Process oats until fine in a food processor
2. Add remaining ingredients except almond milk
3. Pulse until combined
4. Add milk gradually until mixture holds together
5. Roll into 12 balls
6. Chill for 30 minutes

These little joy bombs pack 6g of protein each and will keep everyone satisfied until the main breakfast.

Festive Morning Glow Smoothie

This vibrant drink brings Christmas colors to life while delivering pure nutrition.

Into Your Blender:

2 cups fresh spinach

1 cup frozen cranberries

1 ripe banana

1½ cups almond milk

1 scoop vanilla protein powder

1 tablespoon honey (optional)

Ice to perfect consistency

Blend until smooth and creamy. The natural sweetness from banana balances the tart cranberries perfectly, while spinach provides iron and vitamins invisibly.

Christmas Morning Show-Stoppers

These recipes are worth waking up early for – they're that special.

Gingerbread Protein Pancakes

This recipe transforms a holiday favorite into a protein-packed breakfast that'll make your kitchen smell like Christmas morning should.

For Your Perfect Pancakes:

1 cup oat flour

2 scoops vanilla protein powder

2 eggs

1 cup unsweetened almond milk

2 tablespoons blackstrap molasses

1 teaspoon each: ginger, cinnamon

1/4 teaspoon each: nutmeg, cloves

2 teaspoons baking powder

Pinch of sea salt

The Secret to Fluffy Success:

1. Whisk dry ingredients first

2. Combine wet ingredients separately

3. Fold together gently – don't overmix!

4. Let batter rest 5 minutes

5. Cook on medium heat until bubbles form

6. Flip once and cook until golden

Top with Greek yogurt, maple syrup, and pomegranate seeds for a festive touch.

Make-Ahead Breakfast Casseroles

Heavenly Holiday Strata

This make-ahead miracle will become your new Christmas tradition.

Your Ingredient List:

8 slices whole grain bread, cubed

1 pound turkey sausage, crumbled and cooked

2 cups spinach, wilted

1 red bell pepper, diced

8 eggs

2 cups unsweetened almond milk

1 teaspoon each: thyme, rosemary

1/2 cup goat cheese

Sea salt and pepper to taste

Evening Before Magic:

1. Layer bread, sausage, vegetables in a baking dish
2. Whisk eggs, milk, herbs
3. Pour over layers
4. Top with cheese
5. Cover and refrigerate overnight

Morning Glory:

1. Remove from fridge 30 minutes before baking
2. Bake at 350°F for 45-50 minutes until golden
3. Let rest 10 minutes before serving

Holiday Brunch Party Pleasers

Build-Your-Own Breakfast Bowl Bar

This interactive experience lets everyone create their perfect breakfast while you enjoy the morning too.

Set Out:

- Warm quinoa cooked in cinnamon-spiced almond milk

- Greek yogurt
- Roasted nuts and seeds
- Fresh berries and pomegranate seeds
- Honey and maple syrup
- Homemade granola
- Warm spiced apples

Success Tips:
- Prep all ingredients the night before
- Keep quinoa warm in a slow cooker
- Label each item with creative name cards
- Include suggested combinations for inspiration

The Beauty of Balance:
Guide guests to create balanced bowls with:
- 1/2 cup grain base
- 1/2 cup protein (Greek yogurt)
- 1/4 cup nuts/seeds
- 1/2 cup fruits
- Drizzle of natural sweetener

Pro Tips for Christmas Morning Success:
- Prep as much as possible the night before
- Set a festive atmosphere with holiday music and scented candles
- Keep serving dishes warm in the oven on low

- Have food-safe containers ready for guests to take extras home
- Remember to enjoy the morning yourself!

Remember, these recipes aren't just about nutrition – they're about creating moments that become memories. Each dish has been tested multiple times to ensure your success, and the ingredients are chosen to provide sustained energy for your celebrations.

Next, we'll explore festive appetizers that keep the joy flowing through your holiday gatherings. But first, take a moment to plan which of these breakfast options will grace your Christmas morning table. Your future self will thank you for this gift of preparation and nourishment.

Chapter 4

Festive Appetizers & Small Bites

The art of holiday entertaining lies in those magical moments before the main meal – when conversation flows, laughter fills the air, and delicious small bites keep everyone satisfied without spoiling their appetite. Let's transform traditional holiday appetizers into nutritious crowd-pleasers that will have your guests asking for recipes.

If you're enjoying this book, please consider leaving a review when you finish. Your feedback is helping others find the book and reach those who could benefit from it. Your support is truly appreciated!

Protein-Rich Party Starters

These satisfying bites help prevent the blood sugar rollercoaster that often leads to holiday overindulgence.

Herbed Turkey Meatballs with Cranberry Glaze

Makes 24 meatballs | **Prep time:** 15 minutes | **Cook time:** 20 minutes

For the meatballs:

1 pound lean ground turkey

1/4 cup almond flour

1 egg

2 cloves garlic, minced

1 tablespoon fresh rosemary, finely chopped

1 tablespoon fresh thyme leaves

1/2 teaspoon sea salt

1/4 teaspoon black pepper

For the glaze:

1 cup fresh cranberries

2 tablespoons honey

1/4 cup orange juice

Pinch of cinnamon

Method:

1. Combine meatball ingredients gently – don't overmix

2. Form into 1-inch balls

3. Bake at 375°F for 20 minutes

4. Meanwhile, simmer glaze ingredients until cranberries pop and sauce thickens

5. Brush meatballs with glaze before serving

Smoked Salmon Cucumber Rounds

The perfect protein-rich, no-cook appetizer that looks elegant with minimal effort.

You'll need:

2 English cucumbers

8 ounces smoked salmon

8 ounces cream cheese, softened

Fresh dill

Cracked black pepper

Lemon zest

Create by:

1. Slice cucumbers into 1/4-inch rounds

2. Mix cream cheese with dill and lemon zest

3. Top each round with a dollop of cream cheese mixture

4. Crown with smoked salmon and fresh dill

5. Finish with cracked pepper

Vegetable-Based Holiday Canapés

Let's make vegetables the star with these irresistible bites that even kids will love.

Roasted Rainbow Cherry Tomato Tarts

A beautiful appetizer that's naturally sweet and packed with lycopene.

For the tarts:
1 package phyllo dough sheets
2 pints mixed cherry tomatoes
Fresh basil
Olive oil
Balsamic glaze
Sea salt

The magic happens when:
1. Layer phyllo sheets, brushing each with olive oil
2. Cut into squares
3. Create edges by pinching corners
4. Fill with tomatoes and herbs
5. Roast until golden and tomatoes burst
6. Drizzle with balsamic glaze

Stuffed Mini Bell Peppers
These colorful vessels deliver nutrition in every bite.

Fill these with:
Quinoa mixed with:
- Herbs
- Feta cheese
- Pine nuts
- Lemon zest
Top with fresh parsley

Warm Winter Dips & Spreads

Who says dips can't be nutritious? These versions pack protein and fiber while delivering classic flavors.

Caramelized Onion & White Bean Dip

A crowd-pleasing dip that's creamy without cream.

You'll need:

2 large onions, sliced thin
2 cans white beans, drained
3 cloves roasted garlic
Fresh thyme
Olive oil
Sea salt and pepper

Create by slowly caramelizing onions until golden, then blend with remaining ingredients until silky smooth.

Roasted Red Pepper Hummus

This festive-colored dip is perfect for holiday gatherings.

Blend until smooth:

2 cans chickpeas

2 roasted red peppers
3 tablespoons tahini
2 cloves garlic
Lemon juice
Olive oil
Paprika
Cumin

Smart Snacking Strategies

Success lies not just in what you serve, but how you serve it. Here's how to set up your appetizer spread for mindful enjoyment:

The Perfect Appetizer Timeline
- **2 hours before gathering:** Prep cold items
- **1 hour before:** Begin warming dishes
- **30 minutes before:** Final assembly
- **During party:** Rotate fresh items every hour

Strategic Setup Tips
1. Place healthier options at eye level
2. Use smaller serving plates
3. Keep hot items warm in a slow cooker
4. Provide small plates and cocktail napkins
5. Position conversation areas away from food

Portion Control Made Easy
- Use endive leaves as natural serving vessels
- Provide small appetizer picks
- Pre-portion dips into individual cups
- Create "one-bite" portions

Make-Ahead Magic
Most of these recipes can be prepped in advance:
- Meatballs can be rolled and frozen raw
- Dips improve with time in the fridge
- Vegetable bases can be cut and stored in water
- Assemble delicate items just before serving

Pro Tips for Success:
- Keep backup portions in the fridge
- Have extra serving utensils ready
- Label items for guests with dietary restrictions
- Include a mix of temperatures and textures
- Always provide vegetarian options

Remember, appetizers set the tone for your entire gathering. By offering these nutritious, delicious options, you're helping everyone start the celebration on the right foot. These recipes prove that healthy choices can be the most festive ones at your holiday party.

Next up, we'll explore main courses that continue this theme of nourishing indulgence. But first, decide which of these appetizers will grace your holiday spread – your guests will thank you for caring about both their enjoyment and their wellbeing.

Chapter 5

Main Course Magic

The holiday table, with its centerpiece dish commanding attention, holds more than just food—it cradles traditions, memories, and the promise of good health. In this chapter, we'll transform classic Christmas mains into nutritious masterpieces that honor both tradition and well-being.

Lean Protein Centerpieces

The secret to a satisfying yet healthy holiday meal lies in choosing the right protein. Let's explore options that deliver flavor without excess calories.

Herb-Crusted Turkey Breast

Prep Time: 20 minutes | **Cook Time:** 1 hour 15 minutes | **Serves:** 8

Transform your holiday turkey with this herb-crusted preparation that locks in moisture while keeping fat content minimal.

Ingredients:

- 4-pound turkey breast, skin removed

- 2 tablespoons olive oil
- 3 tablespoons fresh rosemary, finely chopped
- 2 tablespoons fresh thyme leaves
- 2 tablespoons fresh sage, minced
- 4 cloves garlic, minced
- 1 tablespoon lemon zest
- 1 teaspoon black pepper
- 2 teaspoons sea salt

Instructions:
1. Preheat the oven to 375°F (190°C).
2. Pat turkey breast dry with paper towels.
3. Mix herbs, garlic, lemon zest, salt, and pepper with olive oil to form a paste.
4. Rub herb mixture all over turkey breast.
5. Place on a roasting rack in a pan.
6. Roast for approximately 20 minutes per pound, until internal temperature reaches 165°F (74°C).
7. Let rest 15 minutes before slicing.

Nutritional Information (per serving):
- **Calories:** 280
- **Protein:** 48g
- **Fat:** 8g
- **Carbohydrates:** 2g
- **Fiber:** 1g

- **Sodium:** 420mg

Maple-Glazed Salmon with Pecans
Prep Time: 15 minutes | **Cook Time:** 20 minutes |
Serves: 6

Ingredients:
- 2 pounds wild-caught salmon filet
- 2 tablespoons pure maple syrup
- 2 tablespoons Dijon mustard
- ¼ cup crushed pecans
- 1 tablespoon fresh dill
- 1 lemon, juiced
- ½ teaspoon sea salt
- ¼ teaspoon black pepper

Instructions:
1. Preheat the oven to 400°F (200°C).
2. Place salmon on a parchment-lined baking sheet.
3. Whisk together maple syrup, mustard, lemon juice, salt, and pepper.
4. Brush mixture over salmon.
5. Sprinkle with crushed pecans and dill.
6. Bake for 18-20 minutes until the fish flakes easily.
7. Garnish with additional dill if desired.

Nutritional Information (per serving):
- **Calories:** 290
- **Protein:** 34g
- **Fat:** 15g
- **Carbohydrates:** 6g
- **Fiber:** 1g
- **Sodium:** 280mg

Plant-Based Holiday Roasts

Mushroom Wellington

Prep Time: 45 minutes | **Cook Time:** 40 minutes |
Serves: 8

Ingredients:
For the Filling:
- 2 pounds portobello mushrooms, sliced
- 1 cup chestnuts, roasted and chopped
- 2 cups fresh spinach
- 1 large onion, finely diced
- 4 cloves garlic, minced
- 2 tablespoons fresh thyme
- 1 tablespoon olive oil
- 1 tablespoon soy sauce
- ½ cup breadcrumbs (whole wheat)
- Salt and pepper to taste

For the Pastry:
- 1 sheet whole wheat puff pastry
- 1 egg (for egg wash) or plant-based milk for vegan option
- Sesame seeds for garnish

Instructions:
1. Sauté onions in olive oil until translucent (5-7 minutes).
2. Add mushrooms, garlic, and thyme. Cook until moisture evaporates (15 minutes).
3. Add spinach, chestnuts, and soy sauce. Cook for 3 minutes.
4. Mix in breadcrumbs. Cool completely.
5. Roll out pastry, place filling in center.
6. Fold pastry over filling, seal edges.
7. Brush with egg wash or plant milk, sprinkle with seeds.
8. Bake at 400°F for 35-40 minutes until golden.

Nutritional Information (per serving):
- **Calories:** 320
- **Protein:** 12g
- **Fat:** 18g
- **Carbohydrates:** 32g

- **Fiber:** 5g
- **Sodium:** 350mg

Quinoa-Stuffed Butternut Squash
Prep Time: 30 minutes | **Cook Time:** 45 minutes | **Serves:** 6

Ingredients:
- 3 medium butternut squash, halved lengthwise
- 1½ cups quinoa, rinsed
- 1 cup dried cranberries
- 1 cup pecans, chopped
- 2 tablespoons olive oil
- 1 onion, diced
- 3 celery stalks, diced
- 2 tablespoons fresh sage
- 2 cups vegetable broth
- Salt and pepper to taste

Instructions:
1. Preheat the oven to 400°F (200°C).
2. Brush squash with 1 tablespoon oil, season with salt and pepper.
3. Roast cut-side down for 30-35 minutes until tender.
4. Meanwhile, cook quinoa in vegetable broth.
5. Sauté onion and celery in remaining oil.

6. Mix quinoa with vegetables, cranberries, pecans, and sage.

7. Fill squash halves, return to the oven for 10 minutes.

Nutritional Information (per serving):
- **Calories:** 380
- **Protein:** 9g
- **Fat:** 16g
- **Carbohydrates:** 56g
- **Fiber:** 9g
- **Sodium:** 280mg

Traditional Favorites Made Light

Lightened-Up Honey-Glazed Ham

Prep Time: 20 minutes | **Cook Time:** 2 hours | **Serves:** 12

Ingredients:
- 8-pound lean ham, uncured
- ¼ cup honey
- 2 tablespoons Dijon mustard
- 2 tablespoons apple cider vinegar
- 1 tablespoon olive oil
- 2 teaspoons ground cinnamon
- 1 teaspoon ground cloves

- ½ teaspoon black pepper

Instructions:
1. Preheat the oven to 325°F (165°C).
2. Score ham in diamond pattern.
3. Mix honey, mustard, vinegar, oil, and spices.
4. Brush half the glaze over ham.
5. Bake 1.5 hours, brushing with remaining glaze every 30 minutes.
6. Rest 15 minutes before slicing.

Nutritional Information (per serving):
- **Calories:** 310
- **Protein:** 43g
- **Fat:** 12g
- **Carbohydrates**: 8g
- **Sodium:** 920mg

Portion Planning for Big Meals

The Perfect Plate Method
Follow these scientifically-proven guidelines for a balanced holiday plate:
1. Vegetables (½ plate):
  - Fill with colorful, non-starchy vegetables
  - Minimum 2 different colors

- Raw and cooked options

2. Lean Protein (¼ plate):
- 3-4 oz for women
- 4-6 oz for men
- Palm-sized portion

3. Complex Carbohydrates (¼ plate):
- ½-1 cup cooked grains
- Include fiber-rich options
- Focus on whole grains

Smart Serving Strategies

1. Pre-Meal Planning:
- Eat light breakfast day-of
- Stay hydrated
- Exercise morning of feast

2. During the Meal:
- Use 10-inch plates
- Take small bites
- Chew thoroughly
- Put fork down between bites
- Engage in conversation

3. Post-Meal Habits:
- Wait 20 minutes before seconds
- Take a family walk
- Pack leftovers immediately

Timing Guide for Success

Three Days Before:
- Shop for all non-perishables
- Prepare marinades
- Make sauce bases
- Chop and freeze herbs

Two Days Before:
- Shop for fresh produce
- Prepare make-ahead components
- Toast nuts
- Make broths

One Day Before:
- Prep all vegetables
- Make stuffings
- Prepare glazes
- Marinate proteins

Day Of:

Morning:
- Remove proteins from refrigerator 1-2 hours before cooking

- Preheat oven
- Prepare serving platters

Afternoon:
- Follow recipe timing guides
- Rest meats properly
- Warm make-ahead items

Evening:
- Serve dishes hot
- Package leftovers within 2 hours
- Cool and store properly

Remember: Success lies in preparation and timing. These recipes are designed to work together, allowing you to create a memorable, healthy feast without spending all day in the kitchen.

Our portion control and timing strategies ensure you'll enjoy your holiday meal while maintaining your health goals. The key is planning, mindful eating, and focusing on quality ingredients prepared with care.

Chapter 6

Sides That Steal the Show

You know that magical moment when someone at the holiday table asks, "Who made these vegetables?" with genuine excitement? That's exactly what we're aiming for in this chapter. Gone are the days when side dishes played second fiddle to the main course. Get ready to transform humble vegetables and grains into dishes that will have your guests reaching for seconds – guilt-free!

Vegetable Dishes with Holiday Flair

Let's face it: nobody gets excited about plain steamed broccoli. But what if I told you we could make vegetables the most talked-about dishes at your holiday feast?

Roasted Rainbow Carrots with Honey-Thyme Glaze
Prep Time: 15 minutes | **Cook Time:** 25 minutes | **Serves:** 8

Picture this: jewel-toned carrots glistening with a light honey glaze, perfectly roasted to bring out their natural sweetness. This dish proves that eating the rainbow isn't just nutritious – it's gorgeous too!

Ingredients:

- 2 pounds rainbow carrots, cleaned and halved lengthwise
- 2 tablespoons olive oil
- 1 tablespoon honey
- 4 sprigs fresh thyme
- 3 cloves garlic, minced
- 1 teaspoon sea salt
- ½ teaspoon black pepper
- ¼ cup fresh parsley, chopped
- 2 tablespoons pumpkin seeds (optional)

Instructions:

1. Preheat the oven to 425°F (220°C).
2. Toss carrots with olive oil, garlic, salt, and pepper.
3. Arrange in a single layer on a baking sheet.
4. Roast 20 minutes, turning halfway.
5. Drizzle with honey, sprinkle with thyme.
6. Roast for an additional 5 minutes until caramelized.
7. Garnish with parsley and pumpkin seeds.

Nutritional Information (per serving):
- **Calories:** 95
- **Protein:** 2g
- **Carbohydrates:** 12g
- **Fiber:** 3g
- **Fat:** 4g
- **Sodium:** 315mg

Brussels Sprouts with Cranberries and Pecans
Prep Time: 15 minutes | **Cook Time:** 20 minutes | **Serves:** 6

Trust me, these aren't your grandmother's Brussels sprouts! This dish converts even the most adamant Brussels sprouts skeptics.

Ingredients:
- 1½ pounds Brussels sprouts, halved
- 1 tablespoon olive oil
- 2 shallots, thinly sliced
- ⅓ cup dried cranberries
- ⅓ cup pecans, roughly chopped
- 1 tablespoon balsamic glaze
- Salt and pepper to taste
- 1 tablespoon fresh lemon zest

Instructions:
1. Heat olive oil in a large skillet over medium-high heat.

2. Add Brussels sprouts cut-side down.

3. Cook undisturbed 5 minutes until golden brown.

4. Add shallots, stir occasionally for 3 minutes.

5. Add ¼ cup water, cover, and steam for 5 minutes.

6. Stir in cranberries and pecans.

7. Drizzle with balsamic glaze.

8. Top with lemon zest.

Nutritional Information (per serving):
- **Calories:** 145
- **Protein:** 4g
- **Carbohydrates:** 18g
- **Fiber:** 4g
- **Fat:** 8g
- **Sodium:** 125mg

Whole Grain & Ancient Grain Sides

Festive Quinoa Pilaf

Prep Time: 20 minutes | **Cook Time:** 25 minutes | **Serves:** 8

This colorful pilaf brings ancient grains into the modern holiday table with style and nutrition.

Ingredients:
- 2 cups quinoa, rinsed
- 4 cups vegetable broth

- 1 butternut squash, diced small
- 1 red onion, diced
- 2 tablespoons olive oil
- 2 tablespoons fresh sage, chopped
- ½ cup pomegranate seeds
- ⅓ cup pumpkin seeds
- Salt and pepper to taste

Instructions:
1. Cook quinoa in broth according to package instructions.
2. Toss squash with 1 tablespoon oil, roast at 400°F for 20 minutes.
3. Sauté onion in remaining oil until soft.
4. Combine quinoa, squash, onion, and sage.
5. Top with pomegranate and pumpkin seeds.

Nutritional Information (per serving):
- **Calories:** 245
- **Protein:** 8g
- **Carbohydrates:** 35g
- **Fiber:** 5g
- **Fat:** 9g
- **Sodium:** 280mg

Lower-Carb Alternatives to Popular Sides

Cauliflower "Potato" Mash

Prep Time: 15 minutes | **Cook Time:** 15 minutes |
Serves: 8

So creamy and rich, your guests won't believe it's not potatoes! This dish cuts the carbs but keeps all the comfort.

Ingredients:
- 2 large heads cauliflower, cut into florets
- 3 cloves garlic, peeled
- ¼ cup light cream cheese
- 2 tablespoons butter
- ¼ cup Parmesan cheese, grated
- 1 teaspoon fresh thyme
- Salt and white pepper to taste
- Chives for garnish

Instructions:
1. Steam cauliflower and garlic until very tender.
2. Drain thoroughly and pat dry.
3. Process in the food processor until smooth.
4. Add cream cheese, butter, and Parmesan.
5. Season with thyme, salt, and pepper.

6. Garnish with chives.

Nutritional Information (per serving):
- **Calories:** 120
- **Protein:** 5g
- **Carbohydrates:** 8g
- **Fiber:** 3g
- **Fat:** 8g
- **Sodium:** 200mg

Making Vegetables the Star

Roasted Vegetable Christmas Wreath
Prep Time: 30 minutes | **Cook Time:** 35 minutes | **Serves:** 12

This show stopping presentation turns simple roasted vegetables into a festive centerpiece worthy of your holiday table.

Ingredients:
- 2 red bell peppers, sliced
- 2 yellow bell peppers, sliced
- 1 pound Brussels sprouts, halved
- 1 pound baby carrots
- 1 red onion, wedged

- 2 zucchini, sliced
- 3 tablespoons olive oil
- 2 tablespoons herbs de Provence
- Fresh rosemary sprigs for garnish
- Cherry tomatoes for garnish

Instructions:
1. Preheat the oven to 400°F (200°C).
2. Toss vegetables with oil and herbs.
3. Arrange in a wreath pattern on a large round baking sheet.
4. Roast 30-35 minutes, rotating pan halfway.
5. Garnish with rosemary and tomatoes.

Nutritional Information (per serving):
- **Calories:** 110
- **Protein:** 3g
- **Carbohydrates:** 12g
- **Fiber:** 4g
- **Fat:** 6g
- **Sodium:** 65mg

Pro Tips for Show-Stopping Sides

1. Temperature Matters:
- Serve hot dishes hot
- Room temperature dishes should be intentionally so

- Cold dishes should be properly chilled

2. Color Strategy:
- Aim for at least three colors on each plate
- Use fresh herbs for bright green pops
- Include root vegetables for earthen tones

3. Texture Balance:
- Combine crispy, creamy, and crunchy elements
- Add seeds or nuts for unexpected crunch
- Include both raw and cooked components

4. Make-Ahead Magic:
- Many vegetables can be pre-roasted and reheated
- Prep all ingredients day before
- Store prepared ingredients properly

Remember, the key to memorable side dishes is treating them with the same care and attention as your main course. These recipes prove that healthy choices can be the highlight of your holiday meal – no compromises necessary!

Next time someone asks, "Who made these vegetables?" you'll proudly raise your hand, knowing you've created sides that truly steal the show.

Your Holiday Side Dish Timeline:

Morning Of:
- Prep all vegetables
- Make dressings and sauces
- Set out serving dishes

2 Hours Before:
- Begin roasting vegetables
- Cook grains
- Prepare cold dishes

30 Minutes Before:
- Reheat pre-cooked items
- Add final garnishes
- Arrange serving platters

With these recipes and tips, you're ready to create a spread of sides that will have everyone asking for seconds – and the recipes! **Remember,** when vegetables taste this good, eating healthy during the holidays becomes a joy, not a chore.

Chapter 7

Desserts Without Regret

Let's talk about everyone's favorite part of the holiday meal – dessert! I know what you're thinking: "Healthy desserts? Really?" But trust me, these treats are so delicious, you'll never believe they're actually good for you. We're about to revolutionize your holiday dessert table with treats that satisfy your sweet tooth while nourishing your body.

Natural Sugar Alternatives Explained

Before we dive into the recipes, let's understand the sweet science behind better baking. Traditional white sugar isn't the only way to add sweetness to your desserts. Nature provides us with many delicious alternatives that offer additional nutrients and won't spike your blood sugar as dramatically.

Understanding Natural Sweeteners

1. Monk Fruit:
- Zero calories

- 150-200 times sweeter than sugar
- No impact on blood sugar
- **Best for:** beverages, no-bake desserts
- **Use:** ¼ teaspoon for every cup of sugar

2. Pure Maple Syrup:
- Rich in minerals
- Complex flavor profile
- Lower glycemic index than sugar
- **Best for:** baked goods, sauces
- **Use:** ¾ cup for every cup of sugar

3. Dates:
- High in fiber
- Rich in potassium
- Natural caramel flavor
- **Best for:** energy balls, pie crusts
- **Use:** 1 cup puréed dates for 1 cup sugar

4. Coconut Sugar:
- Contains inulin fiber
- Rich caramel taste
- Lower glycemic index than white sugar
- **Best for:** one-to-one sugar replacement
- **Use:** Equal replacement for sugar

Protein-Enhanced Sweet Treats

Gingerbread Protein Bites

Prep Time: 20 minutes | **Chill Time**: 30 minutes |
Makes: 24 bites

All the festive flavor of gingerbread cookies in a
protein-packed, no-bake treat!

Ingredients:
- 2 cups almond flour
- 2 scoops (60g) vanilla protein powder
- 1 cup medjool dates, pitted
- 2 tablespoons molasses
- 2 teaspoons ground ginger
- 1 teaspoon cinnamon
- ¼ teaspoon nutmeg
- ¼ teaspoon cloves
- Pinch of sea salt
- 2-3 tablespoons almond milk if needed
- ¼ cup coconut flour for rolling

Instructions:
1. Blend dates in food processor until paste forms
2. Add remaining ingredients except coconut flour
3. Process until mixture holds together when pressed
4. Roll into 1-inch balls

5. Coat in coconut flour

6. Refrigerate 30 minutes before serving

Nutritional Information (per bite):
- **Calories:** 95
- **Protein:** 5g
- **Carbohydrates:** 12g
- **Fiber:** 2g
- **Fat:** 4g
- **Sugar:** 8g

Peppermint Chocolate Protein Truffles
Prep Time: 25 minutes | **Chill Time:** 2 hours | **Makes:** 20 truffles

Ingredients:
- 1 cup cashews, soaked and drained
- 2 scoops chocolate protein powder
- 3 tablespoons cocoa powder
- 3 tablespoons maple syrup
- ½ teaspoon peppermint extract
- 2 tablespoons coconut oil, melted
- Pinch of sea salt
- ¼ cup cocoa powder for coating

Instructions:
1. Blend cashews until creamy

2. Add remaining ingredients except coating
3. Blend until smooth
4. Freeze mixture 30 minutes
5. Roll into balls
6. Coat in cocoa powder
7. Refrigerate 2 hours

Nutritional Information (per truffle):
- **Calories:** 85
- **Protein:** 6g
- **Carbohydrates:** 8g
- **Fiber:** 2g
- **Fat:** 5g
- **Sugar:** 4g

Fruit-Based Holiday Desserts

Spiced Apple-Pear Crisp
Prep Time: 20 minutes | **Cook Time:** 45 minutes |
Serves: 8

Ingredients:
For the Filling:
- 3 apples, sliced
- 3 pears, sliced

- 2 tablespoons lemon juice
- 2 tablespoons maple syrup
- 1 teaspoon cinnamon
- ½ teaspoon nutmeg
- 1 tablespoon cornstarch

For the Topping:
- **1 cup rolled oats**
- ½ cup almond flour
- ¼ cup chopped pecans
- 3 tablespoons coconut oil, melted
- 2 tablespoons maple syrup
- 1 teaspoon cinnamon
- ¼ teaspoon salt

Instructions:
1. Preheat oven to 350°F
2. Toss fruit with lemon juice, maple syrup, spices
3. Mix topping ingredients
4. Layer fruit in baking dish
5. Sprinkle with topping
6. Bake 45 minutes until bubbly

Nutritional Information (per serving):
- **Calories:** 245
- **Protein:** 4g

- **Carbohydrates:** 35g
- **Fiber:** 6g
- **Fat:** 12g
- **Sugar:** 18g

Orange-Cranberry Poached Pears
Prep Time: 15 minutes | **Cook Time:** 25 minutes |
Serves: 6

Ingredients:
- 6 medium pears, peeled
- 2 cups fresh cranberries
- 2 cups water
- Zest and juice of 2 oranges
- 2 cinnamon sticks
- 2 star anise
- 3 tablespoons honey
- Greek yogurt for serving (optional)

Instructions:
1. Combine all ingredients except pears in pot
2. Bring to boil, reduce to simmer
3. Add pears, cook 20-25 minutes
4. Remove pears
5. Reduce sauce until thickened
6. Serve pears with sauce

Nutritional Information (per serving):
- **Calories:** 165
- **Protein:** 1g
- **Carbohydrates:** 42g
- **Fiber:** 7g
- **Fat:** 0g
- **Sugar:** 29g

Chocolate Lovers' Better Options

Dark Chocolate Avocado Mousse

Prep Time: 15 minutes | **Chill Time:** 2 hours |
Serves: 6

Ingredients:
- 2 ripe avocados
- ½ cup dark cocoa powder
- ⅓ cup maple syrup
- 1 teaspoon vanilla extract
- ¼ cup almond milk
- Pinch of sea salt
- Fresh raspberries for garnish

Instructions:
1. Blend avocados until smooth

2. Add remaining ingredients
3. Blend until creamy
4. Divide into serving dishes
5. Chill 2 hours
6. Garnish with raspberries

Nutritional Information (per serving):
- **Calories:** 185
- **Protein:** 3g
- **Carbohydrates:** 22g
- **Fiber:** 8g
- **Fat:** 12g
- **Sugar:** 11g

 Holiday Chocolate Bark
Prep Time: 15 minutes | **Chill Time:** 1 hour |
Makes: 12 servings

Ingredients:
- 10 ounces dark chocolate (70% or higher)
- ¼ cup pistachios, chopped
- ¼ cup dried cranberries
- 2 tablespoons pumpkin seeds
- 1 tablespoon orange zest
- Flaky sea salt

Instructions:

1. Melt chocolate in double boiler
2. Spread on parchment paper
3. Sprinkle with toppings
4. Chill until set
5. Break into pieces

Nutritional Information (per serving):
- **Calories:** 145
- **Protein:** 3g
- **Carbohydrates:** 14g
- **Fiber:** 3g
- **Fat:** 10g
- **Sugar:** 8g

Tips for Successful Healthy Desserts

1. Room Temperature Ingredients:
- Especially important for natural sweeteners
- Helps ingredients blend better
- Results in better texture

2. Proper Storage:
- Keep protein treats refrigerated
- Store fruit desserts covered
- Chocolate items in cool, dry place

3. Serving Suggestions:
- Use small plates
- Garnish beautifully
- Pair with herbal tea

4. Make-Ahead Tips:
- Most items can be made 1-2 days ahead
- Store properly
- Bring to room temperature before serving

Remember, dessert should be enjoyed, not feared. These recipes prove that you can have your holiday treats and eat them too – without any guilt! The key is using quality ingredients that not only taste amazing but also provide nutrients your body needs.

By choosing these better-for-you options, you're not just avoiding sugar crashes and weight gain – you're actually nourishing your body while satisfying your sweet tooth. Now that's something to celebrate!

Chapter 8

Festive Drinks & Cocktails

Who says holiday beverages have to be filled with empty calories? Let's raise a glass to delicious, festive drinks that won't derail your health goals. Whether you're looking for a morning protein boost, an afternoon refresher, or an evening cocktail, I've got you covered with options that'll make your taste buds dance and your body thank you.

Low-Calorie Holiday Beverages

Spiced Apple Cider Mocktail
Prep Time: 10 minutes | **Cook Time:** 15 minutes | **Serves:** 6
All the warmth of traditional cider with a fraction of the sugar!

Ingredients:
- 4 cups unsweetened apple juice
- 2 cups sparkling water
- 2 cinnamon sticks

- 4 whole cloves
- 1 star anise
- 1 orange, sliced
- 1 apple, thinly sliced
- Fresh rosemary sprigs for garnish

Instructions:
1. Heat apple juice with spices and orange slices
2. Simmer 15 minutes
3. Strain and chill
4. Mix with sparkling water
5. Garnish with apple slices and rosemary

Nutritional Information (per serving):
- **Calories:** 65
- **Carbohydrates:** 16g
- **Sugar:** 14g (all natural)
- **Sodium:** 10mg

Cranberry Mint Sparkler
Prep Time: 5 minutes | **Serves:** 4

Ingredients:
- 1 cup fresh cranberries
- 2 tablespoons honey
- 2 cups sparkling water

- Fresh mint leaves
- 1 lime, juiced
- Ice cubes
- Extra cranberries for garnish

Instructions:
1. Blend cranberries with honey until smooth
2. Strain mixture
3. Divide between glasses
4. Add lime juice
5. Top with sparkling water
6. Garnish with mint and cranberries

Nutritional Information (per serving):
- **Calories:** 45
- **Carbohydrates:** 12g
- **Sugar:** 9g
- **Fiber:** 1g

Protein Smoothies with Christmas Flavors

Gingerbread Protein Shake
Prep Time: 5 minutes | **Serves:** 1

Your favorite holiday cookie in healthy shake form!

Ingredients:
- 1 scoop vanilla protein powder
- 1 frozen banana
- 1 cup unsweetened almond milk
- 1 tablespoon molasses
- ½ teaspoon ground ginger
- ¼ teaspoon cinnamon
- Pinch each of nutmeg and cloves
- 1 tablespoon chia seeds
- Ice cubes

Instructions:
1. Blend all ingredients until smooth
2. Add more almond milk if needed
3. Sprinkle with extra cinnamon

Nutritional Information:
- **Calories:** 285
- **Protein:** 25g
- **Carbohydrates:** 35g
- **Fiber:** 7g
- **Fat:** 6g

Mint Chocolate Protein Smoothie
Prep Time: 5 minutes | **Serves:** 1

Ingredients:
- 1 scoop chocolate protein powder
- 1 cup unsweetened almond milk
- ½ frozen banana
- ½ cup spinach (you won't taste it!)
- ¼ teaspoon peppermint extract
- 1 tablespoon cocoa powder
- 1 tablespoon almond butter
- Ice cubes

Instructions:
1. Blend all ingredients until creamy
2. Adjust peppermint to taste
3. Top with cocoa nibs if desired

Nutritional Information:
- **Calories:** 295
- **Protein:** 28g
- **Carbohydrates:** 25g
- **Fiber:** 8g
- **Fat:** 12g

Mindful Alcohol Choices

Skinny Pomegranate Martini
Prep Time: 5 minutes | **Serves:** 1

Ingredients:
- 1.5 oz vodka
- 2 oz pure pomegranate juice
- ½ oz fresh lime juice
- Sparkling water
- Fresh pomegranate seeds
- Ice

Instructions:
1. Shake vodka, juices, and ice
2. Strain into martini glass
3. Top with splash of sparkling water
4. Garnish with pomegranate seeds

Nutritional Information:
- **Calories:** 140
- **Carbohydrates:** 12g
- **Sugar:** 11g

Light Mulled Wine
Prep Time: 5 minutes | **Cook Time:** 15 minutes |
Serves: 6

Ingredients:
- 1 bottle dry red wine

- 2 cups water
- 1 orange, sliced
- 2 cinnamon sticks
- 4 whole cloves
- 2 star anise
- 2 tablespoons honey
- Orange slices for garnish

Instructions:
1. Combine all ingredients except honey
2. Simmer 15 minutes (don't boil)
3. Stir in honey
4. Strain and serve warm
5. Garnish with orange slices

Nutritional Information (per serving):
- **Calories:** 120
- **Carbohydrates:** 7g
- **Sugar:** 6g

Hydration Strategies for Party Season

Infused Water Combinations

Each recipe makes 8 cups

1. Winter Citrus Refresh:
  - 1 grapefruit, sliced

- 1 orange, sliced
- 2 sprigs rosemary
- Ice water

2. Cranberry-Apple Detox:
- 1 apple, sliced
- ½ cup cranberries
- 2 cinnamon sticks
- Ice water

3. Cucumber Mint Cleanse:
- 1 cucumber, sliced
- Fresh mint leaves
- 1 lime, sliced
- Ice water

Instructions for All Infused Waters:
1. Combine ingredients in large pitcher
2. Add filtered water and ice
3. Refrigerate 2-4 hours
4. Strain if desired

Smart Drinking Tips

1. Pre-Party Strategy:
- Eat protein-rich meal before

- Drink 16 oz water before first drink
- Set drink limit beforehand

2. During the Party:
- Alternate alcohol with water
- Choose clear spirits over dark
- Opt for sugar-free mixers
- Measure your portions

3. Morning After Care:
- Drink electrolyte-enhanced water
- Consume potassium-rich foods
- Take a light walk
- Eat balanced breakfast

Party Season Hydration Schedule

Morning:
- 16 oz water upon waking
- Protein smoothie with breakfast
- Infused water throughout morning

Afternoon:
- 16 oz water with lunch
- Herbal tea post-lunch
- Infused water continued

Evening Event:
- 16 oz water before event
- **Follow 1:1** ratio (**water:**alcohol)
- End night with 16 oz water

Remember: Staying hydrated isn't just about avoiding hangovers – it's about maintaining energy, supporting digestion, and keeping your skin glowing through the holiday season.

Pro Tips for Success:
- Keep water bottle visible
- Set hydration reminders
- Track intake on phone
- Pre-make infused waters

These festive beverages prove that healthy choices can be delicious and celebratory. Whether you're mixing up morning smoothies or evening cocktails, you now have options that support your wellness goals while keeping the holiday spirit alive!

Want to make your drinks Instagram-worthy?
Try these garnishing ideas:
- Freeze cranberries in ice cubes

- Use fresh herb sprigs
- Add citrus wheels
- Rim glasses with coconut sugar
- Float edible flowers

Remember, drinking mindfully isn't about deprivation – it's about making choices that let you enjoy both the party and the morning after!

Chapter 9

The Week Between - Recovery & Reset

After the joyful chaos of Christmas, your body and mind deserve a gentle reset. This chapter guides you through the often-overlooked week between Christmas and New Year's, transforming it from a period of guilt into an opportunity for renewal.

Post-Christmas Detox Meals

The days following Christmas don't require extreme measures – just simple, nourishing meals that help your body find its balance. Here are three days of reset meals designed to energize and restore:

Day One: Gentle Reset
Breakfast: Morning Renewal Bowl
- 1 cup steamed kale
- ½ cup quinoa
- 1 soft-boiled egg

- ¼ avocado
- Lemon-ginger dressing
- **Prep time:** 15 minutes
- **Nutritional value:** 320 calories, 14g protein, 18g healthy fats

Lunch: Cleansing Soup
- Homemade bone broth or vegetable broth
- Mixed vegetables (carrots, celery, parsnips)
- Fresh herbs (thyme, rosemary)
- Optional: shredded leftover turkey
- **Prep time: 25 minutes**
- **Nutritional value:** 180 calories, 16g protein, rich in collagen (bone broth version)

Dinner: Healing Bowl
- Roasted sweet potato cubes
- Steamed broccoli
- Grilled salmon or tempeh
- Turmeric-tahini sauce
- **Prep time:** 30 minutes
- **Nutritional value:** 425 calories, 28g protein, omega-3 rich

Day Two: Energy Restore
Breakfast: Digestive Support Smoothie
- Spinach

- Pineapple
- Ginger
- Coconut water
- Chia seeds
- **Prep time:** 5 minutes
- **Nutritional value:** 210 calories, 6g protein, high in enzymes

Lunch: Mediterranean Reset Plate
- Mixed greens
- Chickpeas
- Cherry tomatoes
- Olive oil and lemon dressing
- **Prep time:** 10 minutes
- **Nutritional value:** 380 calories, 12g protein, rich in fiber

Dinner: Light Evening Plate
- Grilled white fish or tofu
- Roasted Brussels sprouts
- Quinoa
- Lemon-herb sauce
- **Prep time:** 25 minutes
- **Nutritional value:** 390 calories, 32g protein

Day Three: Balance Restore

Breakfast: Probiotic Power Bowl

- Greek yogurt or coconut yogurt
- Berries
- Pumpkin seeds
- Cinnamon
- **Prep time:** 5 minutes
- **Nutritional value:** 280 calories, 18g protein

Lunch: Mineral-Rich Salad

- Baby spinach
- Roasted beets
- Walnuts
- Goat cheese or vegan feta
- Balsamic dressing
- **Prep time:** 15 minutes
- **Nutritional value:** 340 calories, 11g protein

Dinner: Comfort Reset Bowl

- Cauliflower rice
- Black beans
- Roasted vegetables
- Avocado sauce
- **Prep time:** 20 minutes
- **Nutritional value:** 360 calories, 14g protein

Leftover Makeovers

Transform your Christmas leftovers into entirely new, healthy meals that won't feel like repetitive eating:

Turkey Transformations

Asian-Inspired Turkey Lettuce Wraps

- Shredded leftover turkey
- Fresh herbs (mint, cilantro)
- Quick pickled vegetables
- Hoisin-ginger sauce
- **Prep time:** 15 minutes
- **Nutritional value:** 245 calories, 26g protein

Turkey & Quinoa Power Bowl

- Diced turkey
- Cooked quinoa
- Roasted vegetables
- Lemon-herb dressing
- **Prep time:** 20 minutes
- **Nutritional value:** 380 calories, 32g protein

Vegetable Revivals

Roasted Vegetable Frittata

- Leftover roasted vegetables
- Eggs
- Fresh herbs

- Goat cheese (optional)
- **Prep time:** 25 minutes
- **Nutritional value:** 290 calories, 19g protein

Winter Vegetable Soup
- Leftover roasted vegetables
- Vegetable broth
- Beans or lentils
- Fresh herbs
- **Prep time: 30** minutes
- **Nutritional value:** 220 calories, 12g protein

Quick Exercise Routines

These 15-minute routines can be done at home with no equipment:

Morning Energy Boost

1. **2 minutes:** Light jogging in place
2. **30 seconds each:** Arm circles, shoulder rolls
3. **1 minute:** High knees
4. **1 minute:** Mountain climbers
5. **1 minute:** Push-ups (modified if needed)
6. **1 minute:** Squats
7. **1 minute:** Plank hold
8. **1 minute:** Jumping jacks
9. **30 seconds:** Cool-down stretches

Afternoon Reset

1. **2 minutes:** Walking lunges
2. **1 minute:** Bird dogs
3. **1 minute:** Glute bridges
4. **1 minute:** Tricep dips using a chair
5. **1 minute:** Wall sits
6. **1 minute:** Superman holds
7. **2 minutes:** Sun salutations
8. **1 minute:** Deep breathing

Evening Unwind

1. **2 minutes:** Gentle neck stretches
2. **2 minutes:** Cat-cow poses
3. **2 minutes:** Downward dog
4. **2 minutes:** Child's pose
5. **2 minutes:** Gentle twists
6. **2 minutes:** Forward folds
7. **3 minutes:** Relaxation pose

Planning for a Healthy New Year

Transform your Christmas wellness experiences into lasting habits:

Weekly Planning Template

Sunday

- Plan meals for the week

- Grocery shopping
- Prep vegetables
- 15-minute morning routine

Monday-Friday
- **Morning:** 15-minute exercise
- **Mid-day:** 10-minute meditation
- **Evening:** Gentle stretching

Saturday
- Active rest day
- Meal prep
- Reflect on weekly progress

Success Strategies

1. Set Realistic Goals
- Focus on one change at a time
- Make specific, measurable goals
- Track progress without obsession

2. Create Sustainable Habits
- Start with small changes
- Build on existing routines
- Celebrate small victories

3. Maintain Social Support
- Share goals with family
- Find workout buddies
- Join online wellness communities

4. Practice Self-Compassion
- Accept occasional setbacks
- Focus on progress, not perfection
- Adjust goals as needed

Remember, the week between Christmas and New Year's isn't about deprivation or punishment – it's about gentle restoration and setting the foundation for a healthier, happier year ahead. By following these guidelines, you'll enter the New Year feeling energized, balanced, and ready for whatever challenges and opportunities await.

Conclusion

Carrying the Spirit Forward

The true magic of Christmas isn't found in the fleeting pleasure of indulgent meals or the temporary satisfaction of holiday treats. It lives in the warmth of shared moments, the joy of nourishing traditions, and the love we express through caring for ourselves and others. Throughout this cookbook, you've discovered that healthy choices and festive celebrations aren't opposing forces – they're natural partners in creating lasting happiness.

Your Year-Round Wellness Strategy

The strategies you've learned extend far beyond the holiday season. Think of them as gifts that keep giving throughout the year:

The Power of Mindful Choices

Remember how you navigated Christmas morning breakfast without sacrificing tradition or taste? That same balance applies to every celebration in your life. Whether it's a summer barbecue or an autumn gathering, **you now possess the tools to**:

- Transform any recipe into a healthier version without losing its soul
- Listen to your body's true hunger and satisfaction signals
- Find joy in nourishment rather than restriction
- Create beautiful, satisfying meals that energize rather than deplete

Your Wellness Toolbox

You've gained more than recipes – **you've developed life skills:**

- The ability to swap ingredients intelligently
- Understanding of portion control that feels natural, not forced
- Knowledge of how to build balanced plates
- Confidence in making healthy choices while dining out
- Skills to plan and prep meals that support your goals

Maintaining Holiday Joy Without the Weight Gain

The secret to maintaining your progress isn't about willpower – it's about wisdom. **Here's your sustainable strategy:**

Daily Practices

1. Begin each morning with a moment of gratitude and intention-setting
2. Plan your meals while honoring your social calendar
3. Stay connected to your body's signals
4. Find movement that brings you joy
5. Celebrate small wins and learn from challenges

Special Occasion Strategy

- Approach each celebration with a plan, not fear
- Focus on connection over consumption
- Bring your own healthy dish to share
- Practice the art of mindful indulgence
- Remember that one day doesn't define your journey

Creating Lasting Healthy Traditions

Let's transform how future generations view holiday wellness by creating new traditions that nourish body, mind, and spirit:

Family Connections
- Cook together using fresh, wholesome ingredients
- Share stories while preparing healthy meals
- Take post-meal walks to admire holiday lights
- Create active holiday games and activities
- Start a family recipe journal of healthy holiday favorites

Community Impact
- Share your healthy dishes at gatherings
- Organize active holiday events in your community
- Support local farmers and food artisans
- Inspire others through your positive example
- Create cooking clubs focused on healthy celebration foods

Personal Growth
Your journey doesn't end with the last page of this book. Consider these ongoing practices:
- Keep a wellness journal to track your progress
- Photograph your healthy holiday creations
- Share your successes with others
- Continue experimenting with recipe modifications
- Build upon your knowledge of nutrition and cooking

Your Lasting Legacy

As you close this cookbook, remember that you're not just changing your own life – you're influencing generations to come. Every healthy choice you make, every modified recipe you share, and every new tradition you create ripples outward, touching lives in ways you may never fully know.

The greatest gift you can give yourself and your loved ones is the example of living well while embracing joy. You've proven that healthy choices and holiday happiness aren't mutually exclusive – they're the ingredients for a truly rich and satisfying life.

Your Next Steps
1. Choose one recipe from each chapter to master in the coming month
2. Share your favorite healthy holiday dishes with three people
3. Start planning your next celebration with these principles in mind
4. Begin creating your own recipe modifications
5. Keep this book handy as your guide to year-round celebration wellness

Remember, this isn't the end of your journey – it's just the beginning. You now have the knowledge, tools, and inspiration to create countless healthy, joyful celebrations. May every gathering be an opportunity to nourish your body, delight your senses, and warm your heart.

Here's to your health, your happiness, and all the beautiful celebrations ahead. Thank you for allowing this cookbook to be part of your wellness journey. Now go forth and create your own delicious story of health and joy.

With warmest wishes for your continued success, [**Lisa Sharon**]

P.S. Your journey matters. As you continue to explore and create healthy celebrations, remember that each small choice adds up to profound change. You're not just following a cookbook – you're crafting a legacy of wellness that will inspire others for years to come.

If you enjoyed this book, I'd be grateful if you could take a moment to leave a review. Your feedback not only helps others discover the book but also supports those who may find it valuable. Thank you for your support!

Appendices

A. Nutritional Information for All Recipes

Breakfast & Brunch Recipes
Christmas Morning Quinoa Bowl
- **Serving Size:** 1 bowl (350g)
- **Calories:** 385
- **Protein:** 14g
- **Carbohydrates:** 52g
- **Fiber:** 8g
- **Healthy Fats:** 16g
- **Vitamins:** A (45% DV), C (60% DV), Iron (20% DV)

Spiced Gingerbread Oatmeal
- **Serving Size:** 1 bowl (300g)
- **Calories:** 310
- **Protein:** 12g
- **Carbohydrates:** 45g
- **Fiber:** 7g
- **Healthy Fats:** 10g
- **Vitamins:** B12 (25% DV), Iron (15% DV)

Main Courses
Herb-Roasted Turkey Breast

- **Serving Size:** 6 oz (170g)
- **Calories:** 280
- **Protein:** 48g
- **Carbohydrates:** 0g
- **Healthy Fats:** 8g
- **Vitamins:** B6 (35% DV), B12 (40% DV)

Plant-Based Holiday Roast
- **Serving Size:** 5 oz (140g)
- **Calories:** 260
- **Protein:** 32g
- **Carbohydrates:** 18g
- **Fiber:** 6g
- **Iron:** 25% DV

Side Dishes
Cauliflower Mash
- **Serving Size:** 1 cup (240g)
- **Calories:** 120
- **Protein:** 4g
- **Carbohydrates:** 12g
- **Fiber:** 5g
- **Vitamins: C** (80% DV)

Quinoa Stuffing
- **Serving Size:** 3/4 cup (180g)

- **Calories:** 220
- **Protein:** 8g
- **Carbohydrates:** 35g
- **Fiber:** 6g
- **Iron:** 15% DV

Desserts

Protein-Rich Chocolate Truffles
- **Serving Size:** 2 truffles
- **Calories:** 140
- **Protein:** 6g
- **Carbohydrates:** 16g
- **Healthy Fats:** 8g
- **Iron:** 10% DV

B. Shopping Lists

Pantry Staples
- Quinoa
- Oats
- Chia seeds
- Flax seeds
- Coconut flour
- Almond flour
- Extra virgin olive oil

- Coconut oil
- Apple cider vinegar
- Balsamic vinegar
- Natural sweeteners (monk fruit, stevia)
- Vanilla extract
- **Herbs and spices:**
  Cinnamon
  Nutmeg
  Ginger
  Turmeric
  Rosemary
  Thyme
  Black pepper
  Sea salt

Proteins
- Turkey breast
- Wild-caught salmon
- Free-range eggs
- Greek yogurt
- Tempeh
- Lentils
- Chickpeas
- Black beans
- Plant-based protein powder

Fresh Produce

- Food processor
- High-speed blender
- Digital kitchen scale
- Instant-read thermometer
- Silicone baking mats

Recommended Shopping Schedule

2 Weeks Before:
- Purchase all non-perishable items
- Stock up on frozen items
- Buy storage containers

1 Week Before:
- Get hardy vegetables
- Purchase nuts and seeds
- Stock up on dairy alternatives

2-3 Days Before:
- Buy fresh proteins
- Get delicate produce
- Purchase fresh herbs

Shopping Tips:
1. Always check your pantry before shopping
2. Buy organic when possible for items on the "**dirty dozen**" list

3. Choose frozen fruits and vegetables as budget-friendly alternatives

4. Purchase in bulk for frequently used items

5. Compare prices between conventional and organic options

6. Check for seasonal produce for best prices and nutrition

Storage Guide

Pantry Items (3-6 months):
- Store in airtight containers
- Keep in cool, dark place
- Check expiration dates monthly

Refrigerated Items (5-7 days):
- Store herbs in water glasses with bags over top
- Keep produce in crisper drawers
- Use glass containers for prepared items

Freezer Items (2-3 months):
- Label all items with date
- Use freezer-specific containers
- Remove excess air from packages

This comprehensive shopping and storage guide ensures you'll have everything needed for the recipes while maximizing freshness and minimizing waste. Adjust quantities based on your specific needs and number of servings required.

Printed in Dunstable, United Kingdom